PRAISE FOR CHRISTOPH PAUL

I came to Christoph's poetry with a hard hat on. I felt like I should probably wear it, should probably get myself *ready*. If there's one thing I know about Christoph, it's that he's always thinking, always watching, very deliberate, very obsessed by language and voice and story. These poems were that, and then some. They're unafraid. They're a hard fuck, a weird kiss, a sad goodbye. They're screaming at you from across the room. Across the state line. They're honest and ugly and true. They're funny. They watch you as much as you watch them. The book moves from the serious ("It Wasn't Rape But…") to the not-so-serious ("SEO Poem to Get Clicks") but you always come away knowing it was all very real. They're contagion. You come away sick with them. They stick.

LISA MARIE BASILE, AUTHOR OF APOCRYPHAL &
ANDALUCIA

"Christoph Paul gets poetry. He balances that fine line between intimate and universal, in this very heartfelt collection."

S.T. CARTLEDGE AUTHOR OF BEAUTIFUL MADNESS AND
THE ORPHANARIUM

AT LEAST I GET YOU < IN MY ART

CHRISTOPH PAUL

ROOSTER
REPUBLIC
PRESS

For Leza

CONTENTS

INTRODUCTION

Christoph Paul's poems, like any true work of art, examine every-thing that makes us humans. Perfectly structured like a brutal solil-oquy of what the poet has endured or loved, these poems can also be read as rituals of solitude, love, humor or interpretations of pain. Paul has a very distinguished way to approach/transform every day life unlike any other poet (in his words, daily events, sound unusual, definite, and insightful.)

Here's the poet facing his own abyss, conjuring images like catharsis, singing with beauty and subtlety, a modern romanticism that he uses to uncover terrible things or things that have made him the poet or the man he is now, because he is a poet who's transformed, no doubt about it, empiric conflicts into poetry (I am thinking of the powerful poem "It Wasn't Rape But..." in which Paul depicts, with an almost Chekhovian craft, a photographic journey to the darkest rooms of the soul or the beautiful and luminous "My Girlfriend's Cat is a Nihilist," a cat I am sure has to be a close relative to Bulgakov's Behemoth in Master and Margarita, a cat who speaks and walks.)

Both bravery and subtlety make Christoph Paul an intriguing poet, someone who knows what to tell and what not to tell in a poem. His skill's obvious, his suffering's felt, his poetry is here to save or condemn us.

Carlos Pintado, Paz Poetry Award-Winner

LOVE

AT LEAST I GET YOU < IN MY ART

That song I wrote,
my one and only love song,
'Rachel'
is about you.

In the verse, our hearts weigh the same—
when the chorus comes
I don't lean forward
like when we talk over coffee or at the bar.

No, in the song, we look at each other from an equal distance;
both of us smile
like a chord progression
that goes back into the verse.
I know you like my music,
but I know you like my writing more.
Do you remember the Young Adult Novel I showed you?
The one that made you laugh,
the one you said had a lot of promise.
I'm going to revise it,
it'll have a new ending–he gets the girl.

She's tall like you, just as cute and even goofier,
but not as scared or unsure.
She meets my teen-me-character
who has all of my exaggerated flaws
and all the authenticity I wish I had.

He goes through hell,
cause he falls hard for *you*,
and like real life she doesn't know how she feels.

But in the final pages *you* pick him,
you see that *you* love him,
and believe he is the right guy....

But in our real lives,
my passion for you is not art,
it is a math problem I can't solve.

But I try to solve it and tell you,
"there's nothing missing with you;
you're what I've been waiting for...
Do you feel it too?"

I'm 10 years old again
learning life's hardest lesson,
some things are greater than
or less than,
and only mutal Love
equals an equal sign.

You stay silent,
pity appears in your eyes,

your shadow turns into a cruel alligator–
its mouth opening toward you
and turning its back on me.

Answering,
I am less than
what you wanted.

At least I get you < in my art...

THE COSTCO COUPLE

The couple at Costco stand in separate lines
so they can get home sooner.

They have dinner to cook
and Saturday Night Sex planned
to work off the meal.

A night together
ending with smiles and spooning,
falling asleep to Saturday Night Live.

The wife's line moves closer.
The husband joins her
and compliments the dress she bought,
saying she'll look hot in it.

Her face turns the same color of her lipstick.
She smiles and kisses him on the cheek.

He holds her close, trying feel her heart rate.
It's raised, so subtle, but his words mean so much,
making her still feel wanted and secure.

She rests her head on his shoulder.

There's no overflow of passion
to make out while the cashier looks up the price
of an old lady's blueberries.

None of this will ever inspire an epic love poem,
but the Costco couple will have obituaries I'll envy.

20 PACK LOVE

I reach for you,
the way Michelangelo's Adam
reaches for God.
They say you're of The Devil,
But God Damn, do you feel divine—
pedaled by Christians and Krishna's.

You make me feel strong and calm
like Lucifer's Pride,
a Trazodone wet dream,
a stare from James Dean,
till I'm forgetting
I'm your meat
rotting on the invisible gallows…
<Cough>…>Cough>…
Men have died
and literally slaved for you.

But you're Bogart's right hand man,
a Noir Film Flavored Popsicle,
that tastes so sweet.
A salacious siren

who comforts
during calamities.

Yeah, you're my vice,
you're my Valentine;
you're my skinny Virginian
who violates and vindicates
with voracious escapes,
as my throat scrapes—
Damn…you're a lot to take, baby.

But you've been reveled in rhetoric,
that sounds reliable in rubber rooms
where smooth southern voices sway
like George Washington's toupee.

You're Rogue making out with Magneto.
The after loving love, that I love to lie with,
but your aftertaste is an act of treason.

My Turkish Queen,
You ain't just killing Armenians,
but devouring handfuls in the Harems of the World,
while the Camels lightly dies into my final sunset.

CANDLES & FIREPLACES

Candlestick Love,
dripping pink.

Waiting like the Jews,
for a miracle.

But God never comes
for this love.

After 8 days
wicks are whittled

and we are left cold.

Fireplace Love,
dripped in charcoal.

Dirty
and full of smoke

with callous hands and hearts
but always warm,

a fire
that never dies

until one of us does.

DRUNK & IN LUV @ OCEAN CITY

My lady, you aren't here with me in Ocean City,
well, you're not my lady yet, but you will be.
I already know it before it will even happen.

Yeah, I am drunk, and so are the cougars
and trophy girls who scream talk.

The DJ is playing that Tiffany song
in the video where she's dancing at the mall.

You'd probably know it.
You know weird stuff;
I never met a girl
who liked *Oldboy* as much as Lady Gaga.

Rachel, I really wish you were here.
Everyone is having fun,
drinking and dancing
but I can only think about you.

I really do like you,
even with all the *choice* pussy here

my heart is not in it.

It's thinking about when we first talked about Stromboli
and I thought you were so tall and goofy
but yet so god damn sexy.

You just had this thing I could not put into words
and I should be able to because I am a mediocre poet,
but I can't…it's that French term…fuck I am drunk.

I knew it right away too,
that there was something different about you—
whatever it is, I liked it.
I just wanted to keep talking…

There is this chick right next to me;
she will just not shut the fuck up!

I guess she doesn't have to
because she's gorgeous;
she's talking to some guy wearing a polo shirt
and a testosterone stained chin…

He gets some words in but she is bored by him;
curious at what I'm writing,
but whatever…

I like you more than her.

She doesn't have that voice of yours
and I'm missing it right now.

And no, it is not just cause I'm drunk;

it's cause her genetic perfections don't
compare to the accidents that are you.

LOVE SPANDEREL

Could love be a Spandrel?

Natural Selection's subconscious,
the staircase spirals to sex.

Nature's Echo

becoming its own song,
that keeps us all singing along.

LOVE AT FIRST SKYPE

I've been collecting your voice

the way little boys
save pennies and dimes
for the toys they can't buy.

They added up
to seeing your smile
for the first time.

A screen blocked us
from our first kiss,
but not from falling in love.

A SOLILOQUY INSPIRED BY STEVE URKEL

I'm watching the *Family Matters* episode
where Urkel turns into Stefan Urquelle.

It really is quite profound
as it deals with the existential issues of authenticity
and genetic engineering—my major concerns for the 21st century.

You're asleep,
& your body's next to mine.

You're cute when you sleep.

I feel at peace holding you close,
writing this

while Stefan shows off his new swag.

I'm not tired,
Family Matters is now in the 3rd Act,
Laura is realizing she misses the real Steve.

As Stefan, he's still drunk on swag and high self-esteem,

but this troubles Laura
and soon it troubles him.

He takes the uncool gene elixir
and returns to being Urkel,
because he doesn't want to lose her...
it is a touching self-sacrifice.

It's over.

I wish I could be like Urkel
and make a sacrifice to stay with you.

I really want to go to sleep holding you,
wake up next to you,
& get breakfast,
but I have to get ready
for the Brooklyn Bookfest.

I head out & find a cab
cause I don't know how to use the subway.

I don't want to be late either,
I want to try get that publisher
we think is cool

to talk to me.

Who knows, maybe one day
when we're older we'll be
readers there, and maybe
you and I can be
something too.
I don't know
what it is,
but I just
always

want to
talk to
you,
even
when
you are
sleeping.
I always do.
I want to be here,
I want to be in New York,
with you in my arms, dreaming.

LOVE FORGIVES EZRA AND STEVE

(to Anis Shivani)

It's Sunday morning,
I'm on the couch with my girlfriend.

I'm reading a new poem Ezra Pound at St Elizabeth's Hospital,
while she relaxes watching Sex & The City.

The Pound Poem mixes well with the sass of Samantha.
I remember watching this episode with my mom.

It's the one where Miranda meets, Steve, the bartender
for the first time, as he's reading Hemingway.

Whether the Sex & The City writers planned it,
the glance she gives Steve shows they'll fall in love

and The Cantos of Sex & The City
starts the chapter of Steve and Miranda,

a love poem
that Pound never could equal.

Ezra tried to be Dante and take people
from hell to the heavens in *Cantos*

but he never got there.
He stayed in his Hell.

No one is perfect, Steve
would cheat on Miranda,

and Ezra Pound became a fascist
embracing anti-Semitism.

Miranda would forgive Steve
in the Sex & The City film,

love helps you forgive
and Gay-Jewish poet Allen Ginsberg

would forgive Ezra asking him for a *blessing*
in the art form both men loved.

TO RACHEL LOU SALOME

You will never be my soul mate…

But you're my shaman soul sister.
There is a great love between us,
a little on the pagan side.
That Aristotle love—of the mind;
soulful, maybe even a little Christian in its sacrifice.

You will see the years pass...

But our friendship will be a constant.
One of the few things we both can count on,
as you'll read many pages of mine,
and I will hear many secrets of yours.

The trust and love we have will grow stronger,
and you will get stronger.
You'll get even more beautiful
becoming that woman I always envisioned,
when I fantasized about you, before I knew
what I would be to you and what you would be to me.

You will soon meet a man...

He will give you a passion and strength
that I could never bring out,
as every time I see you,
there'll be a look in your eyes that was always missing.

You will embrace it...

In spite of your usual scared self.
You'll say he is the one
and you'll end up writing your best work.
You'll even quit smoking, and eat moderately healthy.
Many months later, he'll propose to you,
and you'll cry when he puts the ring on your finger
because you'll feel truly happy for the first time.

You will be so in love and happy except...

That you will hear less and less from your shaman soul brother.
As the man of your dreams, will find our relationship strange
and I'll notice the look of jealousy
a man in love can only have.
Seeing you happy, seeing you loved, seeing you finally in a
good place,
all I'll want is to make sure those eyes you love to look at never think
of leaving you.

You will really love your wedding...

Your dad is going to dance
the way you always made fun of me for dancing
and all your family will be there;
your mom will be so proud of you for finding
such a great guy and that your writing is finding an audience.
It will be picture-perfect; you will be so dazzled by it all
that you'll barely notice that I didn't make it.

I will be somewhere, probably a bar, happy for you
but wishing I was the one who got say all of those vows.

You will love your Honeymoon…

He will take you to Europe, like you always wanted.
You will stay in a nice hotel in Italy enjoying the culture
you always made of fun of me for liking:
as you relax, make love, and write.
On your third day there, you will be doing your Morning Pages
that I finally got you to do and while he's out jogging–
you know, doing what hot guys do,
you'll get to page three and be interrupted by a room service pisan
saying hey 'scholarina, I brought food.'

You will pay him and realize you miss me…

A memory will come when we decided to just be friends
and I christened you *Dorkarina*
as we got so drunk that night.
We ended up back at your place where we showed
the worst and best of ourselves–
telling each other things we never told anyone.
We talked about love and family
and what love really meant
and I told you that if you really love somebody,
no matter how much you enjoy them,
how much they inspire you, how important they are in your life,
if it meant their life would be better without you,

You would say goodbye to that love…

DEPRESSION
LOSS
&
LONELINESS

ANGEL HAIR METAL

Grandma's house had food and MTV
what more could an 8-year-old boy needs or want?

I would turn on *120 Minutes*
and she'd bring me platefulls of spaghetti
bigger than the men's hair on the TV screen.

In her living room, she had these little glass dolls
I thought they looked stupid,
because all women should look like The Girl
in the Whitesnake video.

I couldn't wait to be sixteen
so my girlfriend could dance like her,
all over my new car.

Grandma really liked going to church
and getting her hair done,
but I didn't want to go to either
because Poison had better hair,
and cooler stuff to say
than any of those old guys in dresses.

They knew the truth:
every rose does have a thorn–
at least that was my excuse
for not helping out in the garden.

LEXAPROTAINMENT

When the medication doesn't work
it's all a joyless jungle

where the buildings are tyrannical trees,
piss stains are the streams,
homeless are rotting meats,

fertilizer, for a world that does not
and never will care.

The Jesus I loved as child,
has been rationed away.

We let Science tame the beast,
but blindfold God,
and lose His love.

In the mirror, I see myself as an Omega male,
with weak feet dragged down by his idealism.
I search for the seeds of prophets
but they've all been trampled away
by the Alpha Males.

Is it my insecurities or my idolatry of perception,
making men mold into mirrors,
and Porcelain dolls walk on water.

Calls
hiss and echo
off elevated eyes.

The bastards are blessed
and saints are sobbing.
I can see Karma's cruel color
glowing only in my conscious.

Lady Justice is another rape victim.

When left with just my biology,
and no pills to fix it,
I always wonder:
am I my mother's fears
or my father's flaws?

TOAST TO THE ANGELS

If heaven gives out jobs
my grandma will
make the angels' toast.

Out of all toast I've eaten,
and all of the late nights
of drunk lust that ended

with scrambled eggs and toast
sagging in great disappointment
because they weren't grandma's.

Like this search for 'true love',
I can't find it; no toast has ever
tasted anywhere as good as hers.

What was it about the toast?
It's just butter & bread.

But she made it and I miss her.

TRANSCENDENTAL TRANSLATION

I'm at the shitty hotel gym.
It's just myself, a forty-something man
who can barely move his own body,
being helped trainer.
.

We remain alone till some cute girls walk in,
the disabled man being helped
onto the Stairmaster flirts out some gargled words
and gives them a half smile.

He turns to me, with trembling face,
"T.B.I.—Traumatic Brain Injury,
makes me brave. Who cares…"

The girls leave and
he shares his story, slowly,
like his mouth is full of marbles
of being a football/baseball player,
saying he was a white Bo Jackson,
and then a car accident happened.

I only listen and see

people with brain damage speak their own language;
they have their own culture,
their own set of values.

They know there is no such thing
as independence– only that the more people you talk to
the less lonely you feel.

HOURS BEFORE THE WEDDING

Hours before The Wedding,
I'm alone in Rehoboth,
Delaware, walking
through the sand
thinking of the
spiritual teachers
who taught me how
insignificant we are.
The sea comes in and
takes the sand it wants with it.
A smell starts to come through
the breeze, making
me miss all of the
ex-lovers who
have washed
away; until the
ocean smell begins
to mix with loneliness
that feels as long as the sky.

THE BOY FROM MILITARY SCHOOL

His smiling face haunts me.
I'm thirteen. He's seventeen.
In military school, rank is everything—
I have none and he is a sergeant.

He bullies me but never assaults me.
He slams me against the wall
and tells me how worthless, ugly, and pitiful I am.
I am too small to strike back and too scared to tell on him.

I begin to believe him.

By my third day in military school,
my sense of self is gone.

They shave my head and the older boys taunt me,
telling me I look like a monkey.

I do my best not to cry.

Willingham is the worst one.
He enjoys tormenting anyone weaker than him.

He's not popular with the kids his age.
Instead, he spends his time in the middle school dorms,
Because harming the weaker and younger
Seem like the only thing that makes him happy.

I learn to sleep.

I try my best to be invisible,
but it only makes me more noticeable to Willingham.

One night while sleeping
Willingham shoves a broom up my rectum.

I opened my eyes in pain.
His awful smile and laugh,
I still hear them today.

I don't defend myself
Because he he'd beat me
with the broomstick.

Why would he do that?
I still wonder and all I can think is
he did what he did

because he could.

MY MOTHER'S FUNERAL

All the nice things
you wanted dad to tell you
he finally said at your funeral.

Everyone had good things to say
about you, you weren't a joke—
you just were good at making people laugh.

I miss you and am happy you're finally out of hell.
I don't believe in the Heaven you talked about,
but I do believe you finally found peace.

FATE

&

GOD

CAMUS WOULD HAVE LOVED BASEBALL TOO

I'm laughing with my friends,
eating the best hot dog ever

as the 7th inning stretch song plays.
We watch a man on the dancing cam

drinking helmet head beer,
fist pumping, getting his groove on—

Dionysus on the diamond.

I smile staring down
at the green field like I am God

loving life, accepting that even if
there is no God

looking down at me,
it still okay—

The Game is good either way.

WAITING AT WALGREENS FOR PRESCRIPTIONS

In the democratic process of line waiting,
it feels like we're all in a lineup
for The DSM-5.

Here we all are: the hurt, the crazy, and the sleepless
waiting to get better;
to find chemicals our body once made.

Our different *ills* keep us in line:
from old men who need Viagra
or the trophy wives who need Lexapro.

Or the injured good looking guy wearing a frown and a cast,
with the Indian girl behind him who has acne
and/or manic-depression.

The bald guy with sun glasses
in front of me is my type—
the sleepless.

In a store that has everything we need,

in a country where to live in poverty is to be rich,
why can't we sleep?

HEIGHT

I am really attracted to tall girls;
I recently have fallen hard
for a girl who is 5'11 without shoes.
I'm not as tall,
I am average height.
I'm not tall enough
to play sports professionally.

Before I became what is referred to as,
a 'faggy poet' and got pubes,
I was a jock and a big jerk,
but my post-puberty height
never matched my natural ability,
and those scholarships and sports friends
became a distant dream.

Today, I ride on the cheap train to NYC
to see my 5'11 crush,
but I am enamored
with a 6'3 brunette
sitting up front.
She's the prettiest, and tallest of the group

of 3 girls with average looking faces
and beautiful laughs
having a fun time teasing, "Tallie."

If she was my height
she'd be with her boyfriend on the Acelea.
If I had hers I'd be on the Eurorail
playing basketball in the European League.

Maybe, I'm not even attracted to her,
maybe, I just want to trade height.

Our lives would be, "better,"
but she wouldn't have those
loyal girlfriends
that love her
and I wouldn't have written this poem…

MY GIRLFRIEND'S CAT IS A NIHILIST

My Girlfriend's Cat is a Nihilist.
She believes in nothing

but hissing at me
near the window

hoping to eat the heads
of birds chirping sweet songs

and the squirrels
who run down the trees.

My Girlfriend's Cat reads Nietzsche
and the Marquis De Sade

hissing at my need to pet her
while she waits for me

to throw the toy ball
she pretends to kill.

Then she takes her catnap,
dreaming of nothingness.

NEW YORK POST 9-11

I'm part Jew and he is full Saudi.

We are both in the waiting area
in the Buffalo airport terminal.

We both need to charge our iPhones
but there's only one plug.

I got there first and he looks worried.
He tells me he is low on power and doesn't get reception
and asks me if he can use my phone to call his friend.

I hear my mother's Jewish voice in my head say,
"He is gonna call his terrorist friends,
don't give him the phone,
he is probably being watched."

I don't want to be my mother,
so I give him my phone.

He calls his friend from Saudi Arabia
who I learn, like him, is studying English,

but running late.
I let him charge his phone
and he talks about how there are no jobs
in Saudi Arabia,
so he's studying hard at The University of Buffalo.

He tells me how much he loves Buffalo
and wants to stay here forever,
which makes me conclude that Saudi Arabia
really must suck,
or Buffalo is just way better
than its football team.

I wish this was a Hallmark Moment
that multicultural teachers want,
but it was just two young dudes
waiting for their rides,
in America,
who have iPhones
and friends
willing to pick them up at the airport.

BEDFORD AVE JEW 4 JESUS GIRL

We walked around Williamsburg after the show, heading to a
chicken place named Peters. Baron and I walked down Bedford
when a girl asked me if I knew Christ. She was an attractive Jewish
girl. I looked confused at her Jewish Star–the moonlight reflected off
her necklace onto my Egyptian Pagan beads. It made sense when I
looked lower and saw her Jews 4 Jesus T-Shirt fitting nicely over her
B Cups. I wanted her more than Christ, and stayed around for
her pitch.

She was pretty but lonely and hope appeared in her eyes when I said
"My mother was a Jew but I don't want to be one of 144,000 taken to
Heaven during Revelations–it just seems unfair."

Baron was less interested in a spiritual debate, "Since you found
Jesus can you give good head now since you're Christian, cause all
the Jewish girls I've banged have never given me good head."

She blushed and said, "I wouldn't do that even with my husband."

Baron nodded like that made sense and asked her if she was married
and she said 'no' looking at me, checking me out, the mutual attrac-

tion happening between young people on a Friday night on the side-walks of Brooklyn.

I could see the fantasy in the smile that escaped her: I find Jesus, quit writing and Rock N Roll, and we share the good news together before the End of Times.

But the smile ended and she asked, "You have studied the Bible, you can read, but have you read it as the word of God?"

I looked at her and thought we'd make a nice couple, that it was too bad; it's like if there was a God He had other plans and I said, "No, I just don't see it like that. Never will. But sometimes I really wish I did."

Baron said, "Come on, let's go try that chicken place.

We left her but I still wonder what could have been.

I don't pray for her, but hope she finds somebody that makes her feel the way Jesus does.

POSITIVE AFFIRMATIONS

It's time to be positive.
It's time to suck Tony Robin's cock
or at least no longer fuck Negative Nancy.

Pessimism, negativity.
They are like credit cards
and I can't handle them.

The debt of depression
is too god damn much.

I'd rather be rich in spirit
and be an atheist Ned Flanders.

Gratitude lists,
They are better
than prayers.

The Communion Glass
is half full.

Pride is not a sin
when self-hatred soothes.

It is smart to be square
when the shape that fits
can cut your wrists.

THE TRAY'S HALF-FULL

I sit here in the college cafeteria,
eating shitty pizza, watching the handicapable boy.

He's working during his lunch shift,
darting around the stale white floors,
picking up plates and trays.

MTVU is playing on all eight TV screens
and he loves every stupid song,
but not as much as he loves his job.

He's present in each movement,
his eyes full of purpose.

The music video ends,
the TV screen shows scenes from Spring Break.

The young man's Zen mastery of carrying trays
comes to a stop
as 3 bikini girls' scream on the screen.

He looks up from a dirty table,
smiles, and says, "Look at the titties,
they bounce;
I love the titties, they so good."

Giggles from the freshmen
and looks of embarrassment
from the grad students
fill the cafeteria.

They stop once the they realize
it's *wrong* to laugh.

Like dominos
they fall into solemn stones,
but I start to smile
watching a happy boy who got to say
what all the other guys were thinking.

Sometimes restraint can be suffocating,
manners & mannerisms
can mask our truest moments.

I envy him
and wonder if there is a balance,
if there is some type of justice.

Is he blessed to not care what people think?
How many of us can say that and mean it?
Out of all the people in that cafeteria,
chugging their second cup of Redbull
or late to take some pointless pop quiz,

Living for the future, living for security,
for their parents,
to worry,
wearing the time in their eyes except him.

He wears his own face.
He will love this job more than any of us will love ours.
He is alive, living for titties and trays.

HUFFING GAS TO FEEL GOD

Instead of prayer & meditation,
I found a gas tank.

Rehab was horrible
and I dared to change
my state.

I felt

no different
from a Buddhist

trying to reach
nirvana

by controlling
the oxygen
to his brain.

You feel peace
or God…

when...
you stop...
your...
thoughts...

SEX?
SEX!
SEX☺

THE GOOD, THE BAD, & THE UGLY OF AN NYC ONE-NIGHT STAND

Drunk eyes are always honest.
I can read what her's say:
you're attractive enough to get me off,
but not too attractive to reject me.

I answer her eyes with a smile,
and stare at her breasts and curves
like they're codes
that'll quiet this mantra blood rush
of need and want.

I'm drunk on vodka & Redbull.

But really, I'm cells tricking the idea
of 'me'
to have non-reproductive sex;

I am Darwin's truth in Lucky Jeans.

I tell her all the right things,
touch her in all the right ways:

my words are chess pieces,
my body is a language—
charades
to make her say,
"let's go back to my place."

It takes 3 hours, 2 bars,
1 diner, and 1 dance club
for her to end the game
where the night is as dark
as our ancestor's cave.

But the light
in her room
shows off a blue nighty
that clashes with her eyes.
I pretend to listen about her PhD thesis.

Twenty minutes later, a condom is on.
I am inside her and feel moisture against rubber.

She moans just loud enough
and I feel the intoxication of validation
Intertwining with physical pleasure.

She comes and so does my exhaustion
but I want to make it more than what it is.
Grunts and moans cum together
creating a sound for the angels
before they fall to hell.

Minutes later, she yawns
and falls a sleep.
I did a good job but I can't sleep.

I never can sleep unless the TV is on.

I hold her for ten minutes
pretending she is all the girls I never got
until the lie is destroyed by her snores.

I sneak out but leave my business card;
if she wants to go again,
but she won't.

I go home to what I know:
sleeping alone with the TV on.

TO NICOLE ANISTON

What Nabokov did for language
you did for the reverse cowgirl.
Your body going up and down
making me pause and stare
harder than any screw
holding up a painting in *The Lourve*.

I watch you cum harder
than similes Neruda's heart spilled out.
Your moans hitting notes
that Motown's songs of love and loss
never could.
There's no script,
that captures what you do,
just a Casablanca smile,
pretty as your Rosebud.

I dream of you more than Gatsby
dreamed of Daisy.
I am Anna Karenina
and you are Count Vronksy
sucking something in me

that moves my blood,
until I'm Stevie Wonder
and you're braille on my keyboard.

You're Camille Paglia on Tubegalore,
Sexual Personae and decadent romanticism
casting a Lana Del Rey spell
when you look into my Western eyes
and I'm lost in your Psalms.

MY JUNGIAN QUEEN

Oh, my blond queen, not a royal one,
but in Jungian terms.
You are my ideal.
You pull me in.

But he is there…

He looks like the dead kid on *Glee*,
The QB who Od'd,
and he is eating all your goat cheese bruschetta.
He eats it fast and sloppy not savoring the flavors,
that's probably how he licks your pussy.

He's got King energy too.
Logical like you, but lazy
in bed and in life.

He can't see you, he only looks at his phone
while you waste your cute af idiosyncrasies
on him.

He's a colorblind boy

walking blindly in the museum
of you.

My goofy little queen,
In a perfect world, I would be your daily jester,
your magician
making you laugh and cum,
and the only time I'd look at the phone with you
is when you'd send me sexy af pics.

Oh. This fantasy in my head
is way better than the goat cheese bruschetta
and they make some damn good GC bruschetta here.

FUCK IT,
I'm going to do it, I am going throw out all decorum
and declare that we are each-others destiny.

But before I can become the star
of my own late night romantic-sex-comedy,
he eats his final bite of bruschetta and throws
Andrew Jackson's smug face on the table

and you are gone,
gone with him,
and I'm left this poem,
and the last bite of some good goat cheese bruschetta.

TRUST FUND GIRL

I think of you on Monday Mornings
and Wednesday afternoons.
I remember your awkward attempt at flirting,
as your gay BFF nudged you toward me.

I liked the ego-boost as we talked,
I waited for my burritos and you drank mojitos;
I took in your scent and smile
with my chimichangas.

Chemistry just wasn't there,
attraction comes in those first few moments
and I did not feel it and told you I was tired.

But the less interested I became
the more interested you were.
I told you I was a writer/
musician with a shitty day job.

Your gay BFF laughed hard
when I asked what you do
and you looked embarrassed

and said, "I go to art events."

The lack of pride in your face
and vulnerability in your eyes
you could not hide, as your Gay BFF translated,
"She's a Trust Fund Girl."

This news took me to an evil place;
I looked down at your crotch like it was a wallet.
The exhaustion I felt and your attraction to me
and lack of purpose in your life could be

transcended
if I went home with you,
became your boyfriend and lived off of you
while writing prolifically.

I need money and you need
something close to love,
since your parents gave you a lot of money
instead of the real thing.

Maybe trading money for love
is the real root of evil.
I'm not evil, but somedays
I wish I was,

because right now
we'd be celebrating
our passionless anniversary
at my sold out "art event."

TINDER HAIKU

Your profile picture
doesn't look like you, like, at all.
Shrugs fuck it, lets fuck.

YOU GAVE ME BLOW-JOBITIS

You gave me Blow-Jobitis.
I lay mummified, wrapped up
in Quicksilver bed sheets
wondering if Cleopatra ever
gave head this good.

Did Shakespeare write Sonnets
cause his Montague sword
was polished with the Capulet fury
you forced upon me?

You made me make moans
that were soliloquies singing
to the sound of your tongue.

I became every orgy in Old Rome
falling into Freddy Cougar's
bed of Good Dreams.

I am a cum ghost now
on a spirit journey
thinking of who got the first blow job.

Was it a monkey or bored neanderthals
that needed something to do during winter?
I'd give them all the fresh kills & bananas
in the world to thank them for this moment.

We have evolved but science shows
everything we do & like
is an adaptive strategy that
helped us survive & reproduce.

I don't know how the blow job
helped with either
but the one you gave me
makes me happy
to be alive.

COMING TO AN AMERICAN PORN STORE

I miss the African men who walked into the pornstore
with their Prince of Zamunda smiles.
Many were from Ethopia and other countries
that Christians and Sally Struthers visited in the 90s.

We bonded during the World Cup
as the non-African black customers thought,
"Niggas not using their hands is some boring ass shit."
But the Africans and I shared the story of Ghana,

they used the word 'soccer' as a way to connect with me.
Most of these men were taxi drivers, cooks, and janitors—
single men who didn't own computers and bought
$4.95 flicks as I made them their free hot dogs.

Only one woman from Africa ever came into the porn store.
She was from Ethiopia, in her mid-thirties, very beautiful,
very married, and very sexually unsatisfied
confessing to me she was circumcised and couldn't orgasm.

She was lonely and lost in America, stuck in an arranged marriage.
I taught her about *American Idol* and how to masturbate.

I rooted for her to have happiness—or at least an orgasm,
suggesting to try bringing a toy into bedroom,

and teach her husband how to use it. I looked forward to hearing
about her marriage improving, but she never came back.
She called only once, telling me he found out and forbade her to go
outside, she cried & cried & then hung up.

I still think about her: bored and disenchanted,
and resigned that she's in this new land
with no new opportunities, with no new chances—
living in America, for better or for worst.

ITCHY FINGERS

Sex leaves me dry mouthed
just like ice cream;
no matter how organic,
I'm still hungry.

Since I was a boy, I've been finding
5 to 15 minute soul touchers,
but they slip out of my hands
leaving me with itchy fingers.

Even when I prayed
my hands remained clammy.

The inner sweat
keeps me cold
no matter who holds me.

Dopamine and self-esteem
can only be tricked
by pills
for so long.

If I hold my own baby,
will I forget myself?

Distant prayers,
with white fences
where Saint Peters
has no hands
and I'm a paint brush
whittled down to a rusty key.

I fool friends and lovers
That I can open some-
thing for them.

IT WASN'T RAPE BUT...

I thought you were my friend,
maybe even a father figure,
or the big brother I never had
who liked to get me drunk,

patted me on the back
and talked
about the love Byron had for Shelley,
inspiring poems

that I could one day write
if I was brave enough to live my truth.
I wasn't sure what my truth was,
you said you'd show me.

You took me to a gay bar,
bought me drinks & told me
to see beauty
and let go of who I thought I was,

I didn't see beauty
in the older boys who smiled at me

and paid attention to me like I wished my father had.
I liked being told I was beautiful.

I slurred
"I'm not really feeling this."
You nodded and took me to another bar
and bought twice as many drinks,

Until I was singing bad pop songs
in the car ride home.
You help me into your bed
and I was laughing

I stopped when I felt hands
rubbing against my stomach.
I was hard, hazy, and confused,
because it felt kind of good.

You stroked me and put me
in your mouth
and it felt ok
but also weird

I didn't know what to say
Or do,
Or how to act.
I tried to enjoy it, but I did not.

I could not cum
I felt the stubble above your lip,
I left
& never spoke to you again.

ART

SUICIDE IDOLS

All my idols
took their life
and I'm taking fish oil.
I want to live, but for what–
to do what they did, but then what?
To be Sisyphus and push my rock until
no one wants to watch me push it any anymore.

Still…I will
keep pushing, I'll
trick myself into living.
I'm Faust and Robert Johnson
with no soul and fame. Only work,
only goals–ambition that is Shakespeare-lite.

Ecclesiastes
2:17-23 "All of
it is meaningless, a
chasing after the wind."
God was smart enough to be an agnostic.

To remind us,

in the end we just
have to live. But I'll always
live with that need to touch the
world & when I touch it & realize
how cold It really is…I will still hold on.

HEY BAUDELAIRE

(For Philip LoPresti)

I am lonely, Charles,
and don't fit in either.

I feel your eyes
in my finger tips.

Do you have the same burn?
Do you get the joke?
You would have hated condoms.

Do you like my rubber prose;
it's full of cum and Catholic-Jew guilt.

Love or whores, right?

Neither us never liked the middle–
maybe the Catholics are right
and purgatory is here.

The flowers I pick are never evil.
That word doesn't mean much now.
Art isn't evil, it's just bored like bees and ants
who can't pollinate the queen.

GOD SELLS WELL IN THE BRONX

I look outside my office window
and take a writing break.
I see a man painting in front of the jewelry store.

We are both making art but we find different truths.
He is selling something *better*
as he paints crosses that have
more beauty than the gold Christs' behind him.

Another man sings gospel down the street
as people drop dollars into his Cross Cup.

The Bronx Christian artists are the lucky creatives;
their songs always touch hearts,
and their paintings always get views.

Their flock will pay the rent
and they're never selling out.

I make art to forget death
and find something close to "truth"
but they know the truth

and their Target Audience.

They can sing out of key,
the cross can be crooked–
their audience will still like it.
They'll still find it beautiful
And they'll still pay for it.

I wish I was saved,
and not sneaking around,
working for Cesar
to trick myself into thinking
I'm doing something divine
while still needing health insurance.

They don't need it;
death isn't so bad for them.

YOU ARE NOT YOUR AMAZON RANKING

You are not your Amazon sales rank.
Say it how Tyler Durden said it
to his space monkeys.

Say it the way Buddhists
see The World
with no I, me, or you.

Say it the way the girl at the bar
bats away free drinks
with cold eyed confidence.

Say it like the the old writers
who only knew
paper, passion, and patrons.

SEO POEM TO GET CLICKS

Hitler got Obama botox, with Tom Cruise on a Taliban couch that Osama Bin Laden hid the truth on 9–11. Jihad. As The Top 10 Ways Grumpy Cat told you how lose weight and grow two inches. Small penis? Best Sex tapes add and lose ten pounds. Birther of Iran bombing Syria while Miley Cyrus' breaking ball of Berlin Wall, where the Pope told children that NAMBLA has pedophiles in your area. Until Occupy Wall Street crumbled until Deen racist recipes were ready to go green with reptilian and David Icke. Britney Spears stabbed OJ until Orange Is The New Black Season 4 came on Netflix and On Demand free savings every week until The Ides of March were not black history but Jezebel Huffington Posted on Facebook how to speak fluent Chinese who told communist chickens to have antibiotics that children in Africa gave to Pirates of the Caribbean as Orlando Bloom chanted Nam Myoho Renge Kyo until meditation told David Lynch where on Mullholand Drive he gave independent lesbians the right to marry and be covered under Obamacare until Ted Cruz sent them to Canada where the Trailer Park Boys told the mayor of Toronto to not take Marion Berry's crack and change the name of The Redskins. As Small Pox on blankets that you can knit in ten minutes or less or on Craigslist for singles serving plates that Ikea dropped on the floor of Lourve that the DiVinci Code showed Jesus walking in Mexico and raptured Tequila that Mel Gibson sold to the Jews that the Palestinians lost and thought Zionists where the meaning of the Matrix but the sequels of the Godfather made Marlon Brando can't believe it is not butter of Fabio's top 3 romantic novels on Amazon that Sting saved and Bono dated Bill Clinton's intern in the IRA that Fox News said MSNBC said Bill O'Reily dated a lesbian vibrator that wind power would use to help offshore drilling that Donald Trump pussy grabbed until Google Googled itself and read this poem and tagged itself labeling it post-post-post modern.

WRITING AT YOUR DAY JOB

Each sentence is a trail,
and they're gonna catch you.
One too many similes
is going to lead you
to a firing squad.

You follow your dreams
but have dreams of getting fired;
every excuse gets used,
until you get a performance eval.

Your work gets better,
and your work for them
gets worse.

You become Ahab
the white of the screen calls you,
to catch that right sentence,
but when they catch you,
you'll walk the unemployment line.

GOD'S COFFEE BREAK

Every inch you count–
measuring,
looking for
angles,
symmetry,
dominance,
and perfection,
hoping you aren't
a failed biology project.
Or God's Coffee Break,
His cram session, a pop
quiz with white out.
But if He is absent
then we are
art projects
wanting
a fetch-
ing
face
want-
ing

to be
purchased
and hung up
before you die.

CLOSER TO GOD, CLOSER TO LOVE

Maybe, we'll all end up with nothing.
We'll be the fools
whose passion
leads them to being the joker card
of life.

We'll be a number,
a spade, or a heart
that should have stayed
at the bottom
of the deck.

When it's all done, we will turn into
tarot cards and archetypes.

Walking folklore, where each step we made
was a tail only Fortuna saw.

Some will be Comedies
that pleased Apollo;
the rest,
Tragedies

that pleased Dionysus
but in our final breath
we will feel something
close to God
something
close to
Love...

AT LEAST I GET YOU > IN MY ART

I am the grey bird
Whose feathers you paint and kiss
Bright with your love
Dusting off the death
Of God, my father, mother,
And the balloon that keeps me from flying.

Your smile turns me into Nabokov's favorite butterfly.
You take my fallen feathers,
Dip the edge in Amor Fati's blood
And write us a sonnet.

I teach you to sing
And you teach me to live and die
In the moment our mouths meet
Giving birth to hymns
That are dirty and holy.

I taste your feet like Jesus,
Worshiping the altar between your legs
Full of Aphrodite tears
And Apollo's heartaches.

I suck the poison
Out of your heart
Spitting into Mother Mary's eyes
And she forgives and blesses both of us.

I have found something like God
In our touch,
Our fingers turn our bodies into pages
And the pages become part of our bodies.

After a day of labor,
I lay by your side
And let the violin strings of your hair
Sing me to sleep,
Dreaming of dying together
As art, love, and soul.

ACKNOWLEDGMENTS

Leza Cantoral, thank you for being in my life and giving me the inspiration to complete this collection. Thank you Carlos Pintado, Lisa Marie-Basile, S.T. Cartledge, and Philip LoPresti for giving me encouragement and early eyes on this collection. Joel Amat Güell, you are so fun to work with and inspiring and I cherish this book cover. My homegirl Lynn Davis, you gave me a safe place to be emo besides writing poetry. My bro Brad for always being a good friend and taking me to Ocean City. LowRes Wünderbred, your shorts are funny af and have balls, and inspiring me to not give fuck and just write. My guitar player Sean, your father John, and your mom Linda who have always encouraged me to keep writing poetry and making art. Rachel Altizio, for inspiring me to go deeper in my work. Michale Kazepis for always being a great friend and fellow publisher/writer. My cats for reminding that unconditional love exists. And thank you to all you who have been there for me when life felt like it had no meaning and or purpose, you know who you are.

Christoph Paul is an award-winning humor author and musician. He writes non-fiction, YA, Bizarro, horror, and poetry including: The Passion of the Christoph, Great White House Volume 1 & 2, Slasher Camp for Nerd Dorks, A Confederacy of Hot Dogs, and Horror Film Poems. He is the head editor for CLASH Books and edited the anthologies Walk Hand in Hand Into Extinction: Stories Inspired by True Detective and This Book Ain't Nut-tin to F*%k With: A Wu-Tang Tribute Anthology. He lives for pickleball, playing songs, and watching bad TV with his wife Leza and their two kitties.

Made in the USA
Columbia, SC
24 March 2019